I Am Good and Ready

Step Into Your Joy

Rev. Economy F. McGee Jackson

Copyright © 2022 by Economy F. McGee Jackson

All rights reserved. No part of this book may be reproduced or transmitted in any form or by any means without written permission from the author.

ISBN: 979-8-9873894-0-9

Printed in the United States of America an Imprint of The Refreshing Center

Front and Back Cover Photography By:
MistuhWill's Phunky Photography
MistuhWill.com

Published By:
The Refreshing Center
P.O. Box 160193
Atlanta, GA 30316

This book is dedicated to the memory of

My Mother Georgetta McGee
2/2/1938 – 7/19/1995

My Son Edward Jay Jackson, III
12/04/1991 – 06/23/2012

My Father Johnny Robinson
6/2/1931 – 9/5/2021

It's because of you, each day I wake,

with the grace of God, and I can

"Step Into My Joy"

CONTENTS

Acknowledgments

Introduction

1 The Early Years   Pg 8

2 Finding My Way   Pg 17

3 Forever Jay's Mom   Pg 25

4 Choosing Joy   Pg 35

5 Financial Freedom   Pg 44

6 Next Steps   Pg 48

7 Reflections   Pg 49

8 Photographs   Pg 51

ACKNOWLEDGMENTS

To all that have been with me in my journey of Life
Thank You!

To All of the members and supporters of
The Refreshing Center
Thank You!

To all of my friends and coworkers near and far.
If you have ever sent me a text, phone call, a card,
made me laugh, or said a prayer
Thank You!

To the Sister Wives. For the late-night calls, text
messages, and video chats
Thank You!

To all of Jay's friends that continue to call or reach
out to check on me or let me know how you are
doing in your life endeavors
Thank You!

To my Sisters, Nieces, Nephews, Aunts, Uncles,
Cousins, God Children and Family that have
LOVED me over the years
Thank You!

INTRODUCTION

I often start professional training sessions or speaking engagements by saying, "Yes, Economy is my real name". Throughout my life, I would notice people trying to figure out if the person that just introduced me really said Economy. So, again "Yes, that is my real name, and it is on my birth certificate." William Shakespeare said, "A rose by any other name would smell as sweet." I must politely disagree. My mother planned to name me Ella. She thought by naming me after Ella Fitzgerald, I would be a great singer. After giving birth to me, God had another plan. She was watching the Art Linkletter show "Children Say the Darndest Things" and there was a child on the show named Economy. I am not certain what this child said, but my Mother scratched out Ella and named me Economy Fitzgerald McGee. She did not know that the stroke of that pen would solidify my destiny.

*The Economy of God: The word **"economy"** is used with the intention of stressing the focal point of God's divine enterprise, which is to distribute, or dispense, Himself into man.*

Earlier in my life, I asked God to make me a distribution center of His resources. This book is allowing me to do just that. If you just want a little or a lot more from your relationship with God. I don't claim to have all the answers. But I share stories from my life that might be an encouragement to you or someone you know. *My prayer is that this book helps, you draw closer to God!*

Chapter One

THE EARLY YEARS

I was born December 6, 1964, in Jackson, Mississippi. Within months of my birth, my mother moved us to New Jersey. Two of her sisters were already in New Jersey. My earliest recollection of life is sitting outside on Englewood Ave eating pretzel sticks with a boy in the neighborhood. I think I was about three or four years old. I don't remember the boy's name, but there were times I thought I saw him while living in Englewood, NJ. I remember that moment being fun and carefree. Why that's my first memory? It's hard to say.

My next memory was going to a church revival in New York. The preacher was very well known and would travel across the country having revivals. My mother was in the prayer line, and I was right next to her. At that time, I was about five years old. When my mother got to the front of the line, the preacher laid his hand on her head and anointed her head with oil. After he prayed for her, she fell to the floor. That's called being "slain in the spirit". Next, it was my turn. I stood there watching and waiting for what was to come. The oil was in his hand, he laid his hand on my head and he prayed. I just felt dizzy. I did not fall to the ground. Once he finished praying for me, I looked over and my mom was still on the floor. So, I started walking back to my seat where the rest of my family was. As I was walking back, my head started to hurt so I remember sitting down on a bench until my head stop hurting. When I got back to my aunt all of a sudden there was a circle of women around me saying Jesus, Jesus, Jesus. I could see my big sister and my cousin laughing and pointing at me. I really did not know what was going on. I think they were expecting me to fall out like my mom. Remember, I was about five years old. So, I fell to the floor just so they would stop. As crazy as that sounds, I think back now, that night may have been the beginning of my journey with Jesus Christ. Although I did not fall out, I believe the anointing on my head and the prayers of those women stayed with me.

Psalm 23 - King James Version
23 The LORD is my shepherd; I shall not want.
² He maketh me to lie down in green pastures: he leadeth me beside the still waters.
³ He restoreth my soul: he leadeth me in the paths of righteousness for his name's sake.
⁴ Yea, though I walk through the valley of the shadow of death, I will fear no evil: for thou art with me; thy rod and thy staff they comfort me.
⁵ Thou preparest a table before me in the presence of mine enemies: thou anointest my head with oil; my cup runneth over.

> *⁶ Surely goodness and mercy shall follow me all the days of my life: and I will dwell in the house of the LORD forever.*

As an adolescent, I was not always the happiest young girl. I recall being teased a lot. I was skinny, tall, dark-skinned, I had short nappy hair, and my name was Economy. Most of the children in school had only seen the word Economy of boxes of garbage bags. The Economy Size. Yes, I was teased a lot, but I learned to cope with that part of my life. Even at church, I was teased by some of the other girls. I never knew why. Again, I just learned to cope with it.

At the age of 13, the summer before my 9th-grade year. I gave my life to God. I went deep. I got "saved". My family attended Mt. Calvary Baptist Church and the First United Methodist Church in Englewood, NJ but I got saved at a Holiness Church in another city. Holiness is not a denomination, just what people labeled churches that did a lot of shouting, meaning dancing and speaking in tongues. Some would say, where they catch the Holy Ghost. The rules were strict. I did not mind. I knew I LOVED the Lord and did not want to go to hell. No pants, no makeup, no jewelry, no parties, and no music that did not talk about Jesus. There were so many rules about what could not do, I was not quite sure what I could do.

I started high school and felt so strange. My saved friends were in Paterson, NJ but I lived in Englewood, NJ. I would say I was peculiar. But the Bible states, we were "a peculiar people" so I felt I was on the right track.

> **1 Peter 2:9-10 King James Version**
> *9 But ye are a chosen generation, a royal priesthood, a holy nation, a peculiar people; that ye should shew forth the praises of him who hath called you out of darkness into his marvelous light; 10 Which in time past were not a people but are now the people of God: which had not obtained mercy, but now have obtained mercy.*

Getting ready for high school, I was ready to join the rifle squad. The girls at the Holiness church said, "Oh no, Pastor said, we can't be in the school band." Now that was extremely disappointing. My big sister Michelle was a rifle twirler. I could not wait to get to high school just so I could join the rifle squad. You see, I wanted to be just like her. That was my big sister, and she was so cool. Since I wanted to obey the rules of the church, I did not try out for the squad. That saddened me, but I was determined to obey the church's rules.

> **1 Samuel 15:22-23 - King James Version**
> *22 And Samuel said, Hath the Lord as great delight in burnt offerings and sacrifices, as in obeying the voice of the Lord? Behold, to obey is better than sacrifice, and to hearken than the fat of rams.*
> *23 For rebellion is as the sin of witchcraft, and stubbornness is as iniquity and idolatry. Because thou hast rejected the word of the LORD, he hath also rejected thee from being king.*

By the 10th grade, a guy came up to me and said, "I heard you were saved" and then he said, "me too". We became fast friends. I felt like I had someone to talk to about my peculiar life. Soon, more people in my high school accepted Jesus Christ as their personal savior. In other words, they were saved too. They went to a Baptist church in town. The girls wore pants, make-up, and jewelry. They even went to school dances. I was not quite sure what kind of saved they were, but they were not "saved" like me. Women wearing dresses was based on the scripture below.

> **Deuteronomy 22:5 - King James Version**
> *⁵ The woman shall not wear that which pertaineth unto a man, neither shall a man put on a woman's garment: for all that do so are abomination unto the LORD thy God.*

Think about this, there are no pictures of Jesus wearing pants. Jesus wore the clothes of His time that were made for men. Is there a scripture in the Bible that states, women should not wear pants, or a man can't wear a kilt? No!

By the time I was 14 years old, I was "catching the holy ghost" and being "slain in the spirit" at almost every church I went to. I remember the first time I was slain in the spirit. I was at a holiness church with my Godmother Queen. That time when the preacher laid his hand on my head, I went straight to the floor. While I was on the floor, I heard God giving me scriptures. As soon as I got up, I went to Bible to see what it said. I did not quite understand what it meant at the time. I also was not sure if that was the voice of God. So, I kept closing my eyes to see if I could hear a scripture again. Nothing. I was convinced that while I was slain in the spirit, laying on the floor, I heard the voice of God. I then knew what my Mom had experienced many years earlier.

Another time, my sister Tonnie and I went to church with one of my mother's friends. I loved going to church. Not only was I learning about God, but I was also experimenting with wearing hair pieces and ponytails. That night, I decided I wanted to wear a ponytail. Clearly, I was new to this process. Well, wouldn't you know, I started shouting. I was dancing all over the front of the church. When I came back to my seat, there was my 10-year-old sister was sitting there with my ponytail in her lap. One of the Ushers gave it to her when it flew off my head. I think my sister was more embarrassed than I was. After that night bobby pins became one of my best friends. We laugh about that moment now.

Around 15 years old, I realized that I could see in the spirit. I did not know what was going on. I just knew sometimes people came in front of me and I could see their whole life. I could feel their pain and their joy. The pain was hard to cope with. I remember praying and asking God to take away whatever that was. I did not say anything to anyone. I did not know whom to ask. There were times I had spiritual torment at night. I said, "God what am I supposed to do?" I could not tell my teacher that I did not finish my homework because the devil was tormenting me all night. I just had to work harder.

> **Ephesians 6:12 - King James Version**
> *¹² For we wrestle not against flesh and blood, but against principalities, against powers, against the rulers of the darkness of this world, against spiritual wickedness in high places.*

I know now that my gifts were being developed and revealed to me. But at the time, it sure did not feel like a gift.

Throughout high school, there were people that still teased me and said really negative things about me. Again, I found ways to cope with the life I was living. As adults, my friends Sandra and Jill both said, "Economy you were bold when we were in high school. You were a renaissance woman. You created your own fashion trends". I had to burst out with laughter. I said, "that was my coping mechanism". I told myself, if people were going to talk about me, then I would create the narrative and give them something to talk about. So, on certain days I would wear outlandish fashions. It would be normal for today's high school students, but not in the early 80s. One day my friend Michelle said, "It's you everyone is talking about." That day I came to school in a green plaid dress, like a romper. I had on a light blue tuxedo shirt, dark green stockings, and lime green shoes that I wore as a sub debutant in the cotillion. Yes, I looked crazy, but I gave them something to talk about that I controlled. I guess that's when my boldness grew. It was me and I loved that outfit. Funny how what we think about ourselves and what other people think can be the opposite.

Now, I lived a contradictory life at that time. Remember, no makeup, no jewelry, and no pants. Well, I was a model in fashion shows at that time. I would grace the runway with full makeup and whatever they gave me to wear. Then, at school, I was this plain jane girl, that did not quite know where she fits in.

Now, I had the greatest Mom, Georgetta McGee. God created her just for me. Well and my sisters too. As I stated earlier, my Mom was not making me live this crazy Christian life. It was all me and what I thought God wanted me to do. One week, I was preparing to go on a camping trip and could not figure out what to do. The list of clothing had jeans. I said to myself, "I don't wear jeans". My Mom said, "If you don't go buy some jeans and cut out that foolishness. How are going go camping in a skirt?" She said, "God sees you everywhere and He is not going to stop loving you because you have on pants."

Here is another situation in which my mom had to show me, tough LOVE. Earlier in life, I walked down to Doc's Candy Store on Palisades Avenue with one of my friends. When we got to the store, a man whom I had never seen before grabbed my arm and would not let me go. He was saying things that made me very uncomfortable. When my friend noticed what was happening, she pulled me away from the man and we ran back to her house. She told her dad, and he went to find the man. The man was arrested, and I had to go to court to explain what happened. While in court, I found out that the man lived down the street from me and that he had a knife on him. My brain kept thinking about, what if this had been a worse situation. The newspaper described me as a woman, but I was still a child, in my early teens.

One day on the bus I saw the man that had grabbed me several years earlier. I got scared. He would yell things like I loved you and why was I being mean to him? Then if I was walking down the street and I saw him, he would start saying some of the same things. I told my mother that the man was taunting me, and I was afraid. She told me that I could not continue living my life in fear. She said, "you need to pray and ask God to remove this man away from your life." She said, "the next you see him pray and, you tell the devil you are not afraid of him." So, the next time I saw him, I prayed to God. I felt strong on the inside of me. After that day, I never saw the man again.

2 Timothy 1:7 New King James Version
⁷ For God has not given us a spirit of fear, but of power and of love and of a sound mind.

Chapter Two
FINDING MY WAY

In June 1982, I graduated from Dwight Morrow High School in Englewood, NJ. I chose to attend the New York Institute of Technology to study Architecture. I selected the Old Westbury, NY campus. The dorms were in Hempstead, NY. When I arrived at the dorm, I did not know anyone. Most of the students were from NY. I was like a fish out of water. I had the strangest experience. I felt like I was the ugly duckling that all of sudden became pretty. There were guys my age who thought I was pretty. I remember saying to God, "did you change me, or did you change their eyes?" It baffled me, but I liked it.

For my 18th birthday, I came home for my traditional 1st Sunday in December Birthday celebration. That Sunday in church, my mother gave a testimony about my birth. It was the first time I had heard the full story. What I heard growing up is that I was a sickly baby. An ugly baby. My mother said when the doctors brought me to her, they said, "she has pretty eyes." My mom shared with the congregation that she had to sign paperwork to determine whom the doctors would save if they could not keep both of us alive. She chose me. Thankfully we both survived my birth. She went on to say, just a couple of days home from the hospital, I died in her arms. She prayed and they rushed me back to the hospital. When they got me back to the hospital, they had to drain all the blood out of my body and give me new blood. That is what saved my life. As she cried, I cried. She went on to say, that they did not think I would walk. She said she and my aunt would take me to the park to bury my legs in the sand. I am not certain why, but I guess it worked. I am knocked kneed, but I can walk. I felt the love of my mother and was so thankful that God kept both of us alive.

When I came back to the campus there was a party on my actual birthday, December 6th. Everyone said Connie, you should come to the party. I had not been to a party with secular music in years.

> *Secular music is a genre of **music that has no religious or spiritual connotations**. This type of music is often associated with modern culture. The term was coined by French composer Claude Debussy who said he wanted his compositions to be "free from religious associations."*

Remember, when I got saved, I was told, I could not go to parties or listen to secular music. My mother did not tell me that, but the church I would visit with some of my saved friends. All my new friends in college kept saying Connie it's your birthday. Oh yeah, Connie is the name I grew up with. Let's have some fun. It's okay. So, I boarded the bus to the campus party. When I arrived at the gym, I had a blast. I danced as I had never danced before. But that great feeling was short-lived. On the ride back to the dorms, one of my male friends said, "no wonder you don't go to parties, you dance so provocatively." I was crushed. I felt condemned. I had sinned. I just knew God was going to kill me.

That night when I made it back to my dorm, I was afraid to go to sleep. I honestly thought God was going to kill me in my sleep. I had sinned. I was crying so much that people started coming to my room to see what was wrong with me. Well, it was my 18th birthday and people wanted to say happy birthday to me. But what they got was a crying girl afraid to go to sleep. No one understood what was going on in my mind. I did not even understand. I remember one friend explaining to me that his cousin was saved, and she went to parties. My response, she is not saved like me. I stood out on the balcony crying out to God, asking Him to forgive me. But I did not hear anything back. People thought I was going to jump off the balcony because I refused to come back inside the dorm room. Finally, I left the building and started walking. Walking by myself in the middle of the night, in the winter, in NY. Walking and crying, walking, and crying. I finally came back to my dorm room because I did not want people to be worried about me. This was 1982, there were no cell phones for people to call and check on me. I don't remember what time it was when I made it back, I just know it was after midnight. I was still afraid to go to sleep. I had convinced myself that if I went to sleep, I would not wake up because of my sin. I really thought God was going to kill me. Eventually, I fell asleep and, to my surprise, woke up alive. It sounds crazy when I think of it now. But that was one of the scariest times of my life. I just wanted to serve God. I was away in school. In another state and city. No one knew me. There was no woman on the porch to say, "tell your mother I said hello." That would happen in Englewood. So, I always knew someone was watching me. Now, I had to watch myself.

I stayed at that campus for two years, then I transferred to the New York City campus. I moved back home, and I commuted into the city. By that time, I was wearing, makeup, pants, jewelry, and going to clubs in the city. I was still trying to balance my life as a Christian, but I was also having lots of fun.

During that time God was still developing me even though I did not know it. One day I had a conversation with my Mom about love. She said, "if you were not a Christian, you could know true love." I disagreed. I said, "the people in soap operas are always falling in love." I just figured she did not know what she was talking about. I later came to know that she knew the truth.

> **1 John 4:7 - King James Version**
> *⁷ Beloved, let us love one another: for love is of God; and everyone that loveth is born of God, and knoweth God.*

One of my greatest lessons about faith was when my mom came to me and said, "Connie, God gave me instructions on what to do today and we need to follow what I wrote in this paper." Again, I thought my mom was crazy. I was still in college at that time. I did not think God talked to people and gave them instructions to write down. We began the journey. Step by step she did the things that were on the paper. As we were returning to Englewood, my mom said, "there is one more item on this paper, but I don't know what we are supposed to do." She wrote down something to the effect of everything is going to be all right. Well, as we turned off the highway, we heard sirens. It was a police car. I pulled over and waited for the officer. When he came to the car he said, "Did you know you have an expired sticker on your car?" In New Jersey, your car had to be inspected. If it failed the inspection, you got a red sticker and you had 30 days to get those items fixed. It was past the 30 days. My mother explained to the officer that we were going to get the items fixed. At that moment the police officer said the exact words that were on my mother's paper. He let us go without a ticket. That day, I became a believer. I knew at that moment that God could guide you.

Proverbs 3:5-6 - King James Version
[5] Trust in the LORD with all thine heart; and lean not unto thine own understanding.
[6] In all thy ways acknowledge him, and he shall direct thy paths.

People often ask how I ended up in Atlanta. I visited

Atlanta while I was in college and saw there were lots of new buildings going up. I thought this would be a great place for a new architect. But also, one night after I had gotten off work, I went outside to wait for the bus back to Englewood from Bergenfield. It was freezing cold that night. I had on a skirt and no boots. There was snow on the ground and the wind was blowing hard. There was a store across the street, but I did not know if I had missed the bus or if the bus was late. I did not want to move and miss the bus. So, I just stood there in the freezing cold waiting for that bus in my skirt. I was out in the cold for over an hour. I remember saying to God, "If you get me out of here, I promise I will not be in this winter snow next year." That sealed my resolve to move to Atlanta.

John 14:13-14 -King James Version
13 And whatsoever ye shall ask in my name, that will I do, that the Father may be glorified in the Son.
14 If ye shall ask any thing in my name, I will do it.

I graduated from NYIT in June 1987 and moved to Atlanta in July 1987. No one believed I was really leaving, but I was out! Things moved quickly when I move to Atlanta. I met a man. I started going to church with him, By, February 1988, I was married. We had started having "relations". I felt so guilty. I would go to church and tell God I would never do it again. Then we would be back in the same place a week later. All I kept hearing, was It's better to marry than to burn.

1 Corinthians 7:9 - King James Version
⁹ But if they cannot contain, let them marry: for it is better to marry than to burn.

I was 23 years old. I did not want to burn in hell. I thought the best decision was to get married. I just figured as long as two people loved each other and were saved, then that's all you needed for a good marriage. I just wanted to be a good Christian. There were times I thought I was the worst Christian in the world. Yes, I am dramatic. But had never heard any Christian say they had sinned. I knew I had sinned so therefore in my mind I was the only one that was not getting it right. I was sitting in church one day and my Pastor said he had sinned. That was the first time I had heard a pastor say that and I was in my 20s. That impacted my life greatly. I no longer felt condemned for everything that I did not get right.

Romans 8:1 - King James Version
8 There is therefore now no condemnation to them which are in Christ Jesus, who walk not after the flesh, but after the Spirit.

I joined the choir and began working with the First Lady of the church. The call on my life was recognized by the Pastor. In 1989, I preached my trial sermon. I became one of the Ministers of that church. I had finally accepted what God had been telling me all my life.

Matthew 20:16 - King James Version
¹⁶ *So the last shall be first, and the first last: for many be called, but few chosen.*

Chapter Three
FOREVER JAY'S MOM

I gave birth to my greatest gift. My son Edward Jay Jackson, III was born on December 4, 1991. There are not enough words to explain the blessing my son was to me and the world. From a young boy, Jay loved music. Drums were his first instrument. I was still a little peculiar. We did not listen to secular music, just gospel. In the house and in the car. When Jay was in the fourth grade, he was hanging out with one of his friends and his friend's dad and they would listen to "Old School" music. Jay came home one day and said, "Mommy why didn't you tell me that there is more music other than gospel and Radio Disney." All my life I had heard scriptures that said not to be like the world. I did not want Jay to be corrupted.

> **Romans 12:2 - King James Version**
> *² And be not conformed to this world: but be ye transformed by the renewing of your mind, that ye may prove what is that good, and acceptable, and perfect, will of God.*

The men in my ex-husband's family all had a special gift from God. No lessons they just start playing the piano as children. One day my son asked me to buy him a John Legend CD. He listened to that cd and soon he was playing all the songs. I wondered why Little Jay asked me to buy him the CD and not his dad. I think he wanted to develop his talent on his own and then, share it with his dad. The piano was his passion. If we went any place, if Jay was missing, I would ask if there was a piano in the building. It did not matter where we were he would always find a piano and play. My son was extremely talented. There were times I would look at Jay and say, "God, where did he come from." Other people often stated that Jay was before his time.

When Jay was in middle school the Jazz Band director did not want him to participate because he could not read music. He played by ear. Jay convinced her that he was able to learn all the music. The band performed and Jay was great. The band made it to a regional competition. There were just two bands to compete for the championship. They played their number one song which always made the crowd cheer. Jay had a solo part at the end. Sitting in the audience, I did not hear Jay's part. The song did not end the way they had rehearsed. My heart sank. I felt like everyone in the band was going to blame him for coming 2nd place. I rushed backstage so I could comfort him. To my surprise, he was smiling. I kept asking, "Jay are you all right". Finally, he said, "Mom do you want me to be mad at myself for making a mistake? It happened and I have to move on. I can't walk around sad all day." I was astonished. He was my eighth-grade son living the way God would want us to. I would have cried for weeks, thinking everyone hated me and I was the adult.

Jay excelled in everything he put his mind to. He played the guitar, piano, created video games, writing, and produced songs. While in high school he went to Philips Exeter for their summer program. He found a concert hall that had a grand piano, so he spent the summer as if that was his grand piano. Another summer he was accepted into Grammy Camp in California. He was one of 63 students from across the country accepted into the program that year. There his skills as a producer were developed. For his 16th birthday, he asked if he could give a concert. He put together a band and they were awesome. He asked the high school if his band could perform for the prom. They said yes and that was the first time a student band performed for the Prom. He rewrote the music for the school song, and they performed at the high school graduation in 2010. Earlier that year we had visited colleges to determine where he would go. Jay came to me and said, "Mommy I am going to college, but can I take a year to see where my music will take me?"

Jay had created a DVD resume. The DVD included performances, videos he created, and music for others that he wrote and produced. He also had, personal tributes about his skills from several of his high school teachers. My niece Joy graduated from high school that same year. Since we were going to New Jersey, my sister Ivory who was working with up-and-coming artists, arranged for Jay to perform at a famous venue in New

York. She also set up a meeting with Sony executives. They were impressed with his talent.

Jay was introduced to the owners of a studio not too far from our home in Atlanta. They did not have a job for him. He decided he would volunteer for them. He was there every day on time and stayed late evenings when necessary. One of the owners was a famous rapper from Brooklyn. After about two months they offered him a job. He kept reminding me that he was still going to college. Once he accepted the job, he asked me if he could "ball out" for a month. I agreed, and he took his first two checks and bought a brand-new TV, speakers, and a quality camera for photography and creating videos. Jay had always been very conscientious about money. I knew his "ball out" was not going to be on frivolous things.

Jay started his own company, Haven Productions. Before long he was working with famous music performers. He began creating music videos for up-and-coming Rappers. My child was so talented. When he put his mind to a project, he would not stop until it was more than 100%. He was known as **JJ the Prodigy**.

In May, just one month before his passing, Jay traveled to Miami with his friends that were in the music business. For them, it was a vacation. For him, it was an opportunity of a lifetime. He was invited to one of the biggest Rap parties in Miami. He was invited to be one of the photographers for the event. He called excitedly, but I did not know the names of the rappers he was talking about. I had to call my sister and ask her who they were. She knew that they were the hottest rappers in the industry. He was in the same room with people he had only seen on TV.

His last big opportunity came when he was asked to be one of the producers of a new online television show. At the end of the production, they had a party to celebrate. It was June 22, 2012. He told his best friend, that it was the best party he had ever been to. It was late when Jay came home, and I did not know that they had alcohol at the party. I was supposed to wash and braid his hair. I was tired so we decided to do his hair in the morning. I received a phone call from my family in Mississippi that my sister's baby was born. I was already in bed, so I told myself I would tell Jay in the morning.

At 3:00 AM in the morning of June 23, 2012, I received a knock on the door. My ex-husband came to the house because Jay called and said he was having suicidal thoughts. I looked in his bedroom and he was not there. We rushed to try and find him. Before I could get to him, he had fallen from an overpass. The ambulance had been called and while I was kneeling over him praying, the paramedics came and started working on him. He was rushed to Grady hospital. They took us to a small room to wait. The hospital Chaplain came in to talk to us. Jay's Godfather and my Pastor at the time met us at the hospital. We were all praying. By 6:00 AM the doctors came in to tell us that my only child, my 20-year-old son had passed away. That moment was the most devasting day of my life. I screamed as I had never screamed before.

I could not believe it. Not my child.

They took us into the operating room so we could see Jay. My first thoughts were, I did not want Jay to be in heaven thinking I was mad at him. I kept telling him that I was not mad at him. I kept thinking, I did not want him to be in heaven feeling bad that I was hurting. So, I felt like I had to be strong for him.

I have to back up. Earlier that week Jay talked about everything. He told me about girls he had been dating. He laid in my bed and said, "Mom do you think other 20-year-old sons still lay in their mom's bed to talk to them?" I said, "I don't know, but I am glad that you do." He had a job interview during that week and before he got out of the car he said, "Mom we need to pray. I don't know how it works but I know every time you pray something happens". I felt so good that my 20-year child recognized my prayer life and relationship with God. Wednesday morning, he came to me to tell me about a dream he had. He told me that he saw himself running and bad people were chasing him. He said three different groups of people were chasing him, but he kept dodging them. He said he came to an escalator and at the top was me waving a white flag saying, "Jay, you made it, Jay, you made it." As I stood there, I was thinking the dream meant I was about to die. If I was at the top of the escalator, then I was already in heaven. Then he said, "Mom I think I know what it means." He said, "I am going to have challenges in life, but you are always going to be there my #1 cheerleader." I liked his description way better than my thoughts.

So, that Saturday morning I thought about Jay's dream. Up until that day I believed if someone committed suicide that they would go to hell. There would be no time to ask for forgiveness. In the dream, I was waving a white flag saying Jay you made it. God gave Jay that dream to let me know that my child was in heaven. If Jay had not told me that dream, I would still be in bed today, 10 years later angry, mad, and not able to move forward. But the magnificent, awesome, wonderful God loved me enough to send me a message. That dream was my saving grace. But I understand now that the thought I grew up with was incorrect. My child had accepted Jesus Christ as his personal Savior. He belonged to God!

> **John 10:27-29 - King James Version**
> *[27] My sheep hear my voice, and I know them, and they follow me:*
> *[28] And I give unto them eternal life; and they shall never perish, neither shall any man pluck them out of my hand.*
> *[29] My Father, which gave them me, is greater than all; and no man is able to pluck them out of my Father's hand.*

Also, during that week, I received notice that I had an abnormal mammogram. I had to begin treatment to determine if I have breast cancer. After four months of treatment and surgery, it was determined that I did not have cancer. But then, my GYN called and said I needed to run tests to see if I had cervical cancer. After several weeks, I had to have surgery again. Again, no cancer. There also were other tragic events that happened in my family that year. It seemed like every time I went to visit a family member something bad happened. By December I had given up. I figured; I was the common denominator. All bad things are happening because of me. I said, "God my son is in heaven and my mother is in heaven. I am fine, you can bring me to heaven too." I went to church and my Pastor was preaching from this scripture.

> **Psalm 118:17 - King James Version**
> *I shall not die, but live, and declare the works of the LORD.*

I cried out to the Lord, "I will live and not die". As I kept worshipping the Lord, the pain and agony left.
The next year, I started therapy. The therapist kept asking if I was mad at Jay. I told her no. She insisted that I was. She suggested that I write a letter to Jay letting him know how I felt. I agreed to write the letter. That night I started writing, but all I could write was Jay, Mommy loves you.

Jay was on medication for Athletes' feet. He had to do blood work to make sure it was compatible with his system. It was only supposed to be for three months. The package said not to drink alcohol while taking the medicine. I warned him several times not to drink any alcohol. His friends later told me that Jay would sometimes seem a little not like himself while he was on the medication. As I investigated more into the medication, there was a line that stated one of the side effects was suicidal thoughts. If I could go back and make a different decision about the medication, I would.

As I was writing my letter, I said, "I am not mad at Jay; I am mad at God." Oh, the paper started filling up. I wrote, God how could you let this happen to me? I have worked all my life trying to please you and you let this happen to me. I wrote, there are other women with children that were not good moms like me, and their children are still here. God, I have been ministering and preaching the gospel, and this is what I get. Why is this the story of my life? The anger kept pouring out.

Then, I started thinking about all the wonderful times Jay and I shared. I started thinking about birthdays, holidays, vacations, trips to visit family, meals we cooked together, his music, his talent, and the times we spent worshipping God and just talking to each other. Visions of all the great times we shared kept racing through my mind. Then I wrote, God if changing the course of time would change or take away the wonderful 20 years I had with him, I am ok. I began praising God and telling Him how thankful I was for the 20 years he gave me. At Jay's homegoing service many people said Jay had done in 20 years more than most people do in 60 years. Some of Jay's friends called to tell me that Jay was the reason that they were still alive. Jay was that friend! The friend that was there when they needed him the most. He was the one talking them out of taking their own life.

Forever Jay's mom. I am so thankful. Jay told me that he picked me. He said, when he was in heaven, God gave him a choice between me and Halle Berry to be his mom and he picked me. How many women can say they got picked over Halle?

Chapter Four
CHOOSING JOY

I belong to a club that I would not wish on my worst enemy. I am the parent of a child that is in heaven. No parent ever thinks that they will bury their child. Especially not their only 20-year-old child. But, on June 23, 2012, that became my reality.

As I reflect on that Saturday morning there were so many thoughts that went through my head. What if I had done his hair and not put it off for the tomorrow that never came? What if I had told him he had a new baby cousin, instead of putting it off for the tomorrow that never came?

Throughout the years I would see trailers for movies about children whose parents thought their child was going to die. Then through their prayers, God granted a miracle and the child lived. I would ask myself, maybe I was not saying the right prayer. Maybe, I gave up praying too soon. When they pronounced Jay deceased and let us see Jay, was I supposed to lay hands on my son and command him to live? Woulda, coulda, shoulda became the torment of my mind.

There were times, I did not want to hear about the escapades of my friend's children. Sometimes, I could care less if they were graduating from college, getting married, and definitely that my friend was now becoming a grandmother. All I knew, is I would never be able to share my story with them.

I talked to God a lot. Yelled, screamed, and hollered. Yes, those were the conversations I was having with God. We say in the church come as you are and that was where I was. So decided God had taken away the best part of my life so I did not care anymore about rules and what I was supposed to do as a Christian. I got into a relationship and started living my life. I did not feel guilty. I was still talking to God. One day, one of the most life-changing events happened. My friend had spent the night. When we got up, we started talking about God. I found myself ministering to him. God was telling me what to say and he was receiving it. We prayed and it was a very powerful prayer. I went to work and while I was in my car, in the parking deck I asked God, what just happened? I was in a sinful situation. God said, "my Son died for your sins 2,000 years ago. Your actions don't determine my desire to use you. I can use you whenever, wherever, and however."

John 3:16-17 - King James Version
[16] For God so loved the world, that he gave his only begotten Son, that whosoever believeth in him should not perish, but have everlasting life.

> *¹⁷ For God sent not his Son into the world to condemn the world; but that the world through him might be saved.*

Tears began to flow. I felt the love of God in a way that I had never felt before. God said, "it's not about you. It's about My will being done." I thought I was dirty and filthy. But God saw me as His beautiful daughter. Now, I don't condone the life I was living. I still needed to make changes. Soon that relationship came to an end. The crazy thing about what I just wrote is, that was one of the most powerful moments of my life. But I could not share that testimony. No one was supposed to know about the other parts of my life. No one could know that this Christian had sinned. As I reflect on that day, no one was able to know that God delivered me. No one could know that God had mercy upon me. No one could know that God's love and compassion were everlasting. I felt like I had to keep that part of my life to myself. God does not allow us to go through trials and tribulations without a purpose. Now, I am not saying that the bad situations in life come from God. Just like we read the Bible and are encouraged to believe miracles are possible. Your life may be the only Bible that a person is willing to read. You don't have to tell all of your secrets to everyone, but someone needs to hear your testimony. It may just save a life!

When God called me to start The Refreshing Center. I said, "God you must be kidding." For about two weeks I was going back and forth with reasons why I should not start this new ministry. I even told God I was not going to start the ministry unless he gave me a husband. I figured I needed someone to be on this journey with me. I surrendered and eventually said yes. By the way, I am still single, and the ministry is impacting lives all the way in Australia.

It was May 19, 2013. That day was amazing. There were so many people that came out to support and encourage me. We streamed the service live so my family in other states could be a part of that day. I had become a Pastor. Not just a minister but now a Pastor. People even started calling me Pastor Jackson. It sounded strange to me. Sometimes, still does.

So, why did God title this book "Step Into Your Joy"? I realized my walk with God was just that. One step at a time. When I wake up in the morning, I could step into a pair of slippers. I could put on an outfit to wear to work. Each time, I made the choice of what I would step into. So, I began to step into JOY. You know how you go to your closet and see all the choices of clothes and shoes you have to put on that day? I realized that life was just like that. You wake in the morning and all the choices are presented to you. Faced in front of you is grief, lack, pain, loneliness, hunger, sadness, despair, you name it's all there waiting to see what you are going to pick for that day. Almost like, pick me, pick me. I decided that every day I was going to choose Joy. I layer with abundance, freedom, love, power, you name it, it's all there saying pick me, pick me. So as a demonstration I would say, I put one leg in "J". The other leg in "O". Then I, pull the "Y" over my head like a sweater.

Now, I may have simplified the process. My joy comes from my continual conversations with God. Reading the word of God. Meditating on the word of God. Having my quiet time with God. Surrounding myself with like-minded people helps to keep me grounded.

My Prayer and My Purpose: *Worship and conversation with God are the reasons I was created, which is my dwelling place and Source of Power!*

> **Nehemiah 8:10 - King James Version**
> *Then he said unto them, Go your way, eat the fat, and drink the sweet, and send portions unto them for whom nothing is prepared: for this day is holy unto our* L*ORD*: *neither be ye sorry; for the joy of the* L*ORD* *is your strength.*

So, what is Joy? (The Oxford English Dictionary)
NOUN: A feeling of great pleasure and happiness.
synonyms: jubilation, triumph, exultation, exhilaration, ebullience, elation, euphoria, bliss, ecstasy.

VERB: Rejoice
synonyms: be joyful, be pleased, be glad, be delighted, be elated, be ecstatic, be euphoric, be overjoyed, be jubilant

Christianity Joy: It is a natural human inclination to think that living through trials and negative circumstances would not be an occasion for joy. Choosing to respond to life's difficult situations with inner contentment and satisfaction doesn't seem to make sense. Joy is a choice! The Lord is the originator of true joy.

My life may seem strange to some people. There are people that may agree or disagree with some of the things I wrote. But it is just that, My Life.

When I look back over my life, I can see God's hand in all of it. Sometimes holding me, helping me, or pushing me forward. What I can say about my younger years, there was a lot of religion and very little relationship with God. I saw God as the mean dictator in the sky. My main focus, I did not want to go to hell. I did not know God as my Father, my daddy. I will say, the strictness, kept me out of a lot of trouble. I was too scared to do anything. The ministers that I was following at the time were not trying to hurt me. They were just preaching what they thought was right. As we grow in Christ, we gain religious freedom and not just religion.

> **John 8:32-36 - King James Version**
> *[32] And ye shall know the truth, and the truth shall make you free. [33] They answered him, We be Abraham's seed, and were never in bondage to any man: how sayest thou, Ye shall be made free? [34] Jesus answered them, Verily, verily, I say unto you, Whosoever committeth sin is the servant of sin. [35] And the servant abideth not in the house for ever: but the Son abideth ever. [36] If the Son*

therefore shall make you free, ye shall be free indeed.

Do I miss my son? Yes, every day. Are there days and moments I just want to cry all day long? Yes.

Psalm 126:5 - King James Version
⁵ They that sow in tears shall reap in joy.

One of the things Jay liked to eat was Popeye spinach. Sometimes when I go to the grocery store and I see a can of Popeye spinach, I just want to fall out on the floor, ball up like a baby and just bawl. Instead, I stop, pray, have those thoughts, and move on with the rest of my grocery shopping. But if one day you see me on the news on the spinach aisle in the grocery store, you will know why.

The Bible tells the stories of God's strengthening power to men and women who have been discouraged. At some point in life, everyone gets a feeling of discouragement. Those feelings can result from disappointment from a friend, failure to meet goals, suffering with low esteem, the inability to overcome challenges, the loss of loved ones, and even illness in our lives or the people we love. When we hear the news of those situations, those words can destroy our very being. The words we hear can make us feel as though there is nothing left to live for. We must remember it was the words that God made Heaven and Earth. A single word from God can give life.

John 1:1-3 - King James Version
1 In the beginning was the Word, and the Word was with God, and the Word was God.
² The same was in the beginning with God.
³ All things were made by him; and without him was not anything made that was made.

For this purpose, we need to consult the Bible which is the authoritative voice of God. Through scriptures from the Bible, we can pick out those verses that are addressing our situation. No matter how bad our situations might look, The scriptures are bound to honor God. A word from God has the power to radically change everything around us for our good. Jesus Christ is a keeper of our hearts and minds.

Philippians 4:7 – King James Version
And the peace of God, which passeth all understanding, shall keep your hearts and minds through Christ Jesus.

Here are some additional scriptures about Joy:

John 15:11 - King James Version
These things have I spoken unto you, that
my joy might remain in you, and that your joy might be full.

Isaiah 51:11 - King James Version
Therefore, the redeemed of the LORD shall return, and come with singing unto Zion; and

everlasting joy shall be upon their head: they shall obtain gladness and joy; and sorrow and mourning shall flee away.

Philippians 2:18 - King James Version
For the same cause also do ye joy and rejoice with me.

Isaiah 12:3 - King James Version
Therefore, with joy shall ye draw water out of the wells of salvation.

1 John 1:4 - King James Version
And these things write we unto you, that your joy may be full.

Chapter Five
FINANCIAL FREEDOM

I lived most of my life not wanting to be named Economy. When I was in middle school, I decided to change the spelling, Ykonomeigh. Yeah, that! I was always trying to create a new identity for myself.

My mom had Christian shows on TV all the time. I would hear people testify about needing a financial blessing and then miraculously the money would show up. That amazed me. So, I asked God how He did that. His response, "I don't have a check book. I use my people to make it happen." I immediately told God that wanted to be one of those people. I envisioned myself picking up a phonebook, closing my eyes and wherever my finger would land, I would send that person a check.

I started thinking about my future. As mentioned, I have a degree in Architecture. I decided I would work as an architect and make lots of money. Then, I would retire and start helping communities. Little did I know, God had a different plan. In my early 30's I took a job at a nonprofit organization that was focused on housing. I lived on the property, making a difference in that community. You would think I would be happy. In my head, my plan was laid out to start in my 60's. Here I was and I had already fulfilled my end goal. I honestly did not know what to do with the rest of my life. My dream had already been granted and I was only in my 30s.

I did not know, God was taking me to my first desire, giving out money. I thought I had to work hard, save the money, and then I could give it away. The next three places that I was employed allowed me to fundraise for other people's money. That money I was then able to use it to make a positive impact in the community. I estimate, over the past 25 years I have been responsible for managing over $25 Million supporting families in homeownership, higher education, quality childcare, microenterprise business development, and creating emergency savings accounts.

> ***Philippians 4:19 - King James Version***
> *[19] But my God shall supply all your need according to his riches in glory by Christ Jesus.*

One day at church, Wanda said to the congregation, "You are God's Economy." That stuck with me. I began researching the meaning of my name. My mom is deceased, so I had not been able to ask her what was so significant about naming me Economy. My original name was Ella.

So, I started researching:

The word *economy* in English is derived from the Middle French's *yconomie*, which itself derived from the Medieval Latin's *oeconomia*. The Latin word has its origin at the Ancient Greek's *oikonomia* or *oikonomos*. The word's first part *oikos* means "house", and the second part *nemein* means "to manage".

Ecclesiastical Economy: Economy also refers to the Church's "handling" or "management" or "disposition" of various pastoral and disciplinary questions, problems, and issues. Here again, "economy" is used in several ways.

In one sense, it refers to the discretionary power given to the Church by Christ himself to manage and govern the Church. Christ referred to this when he gave the apostles the authority to "bind and to loose."

> **Matthew 16:19 - King James Version**
> [19] *And I will give unto thee the keys of the kingdom of heaven: and whatsoever thou shalt bind on earth shall be bound in heaven: and whatsoever thou shalt loose on earth shall be loosed in heaven.*

> **Matthew 18:18 - King James Version**
> [18] *Verily I say unto you, Whatsoever ye shall bind on earth shall be bound in heaven: and whatsoever ye shall loose on earth shall be loosed in heaven.*

This authority was transmitted to the bishops who came after the apostles. In this sense "economy" means, as already noted, "handling", "management", "disposition".

In general, "economy" refers to pastoral handling or discretion or management in a neutral sense.

Divine Economy: Eastern Orthodoxy, not only refers to God's actions to bring about the world's salvation and redemption, but to all of God's dealings with, and interactions with, the world, including the Creation.

I realized my mom had created my destiny. What I love most is teaching people about their finances and helping them create a plan for their households. That gives me Joy!

> ***Jeremiah 29:11 - King James Version***
> *¹¹ For I know the thoughts that I think toward you, saith the L*ORD*, thoughts of peace, and not of evil, to give you an expected end.*

NEXT STEPS

Take a moment and think about your life. Do you step into your Joy each morning. I say "Your Joy" because joy belongs to you. It is a gift given to you by God. The first step, if you have never given your life to God and accepted the gift of salvation, I invite you to say the prayer below.

Romans 10:9 King James Version
That if thou shalt confess with thy mouth the Lord Jesus, and shalt believe in thine heart that God hath raised him from the dead,
thou shalt be saved.

PRAYER of Salvation
Heavenly Father, in Jesus' name I repent of my sins, and I accept you to into my heart.
Jesus, You are my Lord and Savior. I believe you died for my sins, and you were raised from the dead.
Fill me with your Holy Spirit. Thank You Father for saving me in Jesus' name. Amen.

If you prayed this prayer for the first time or if you are seeking closer relationship God, the Angels in Heaven are shouting the victory for you! God hears you and He LOVES you right where you are.

God truly LOVES you and wants you to live a life of Joy, Purpose, and Fulfillment.

REFLECTIONS

ABOUT THE AUTHOR

Rev. Economy F. McGee Jackson has served as a Minister since 1989. She was called by God in 2013 to Pastor **The Refreshing Center, "A Haven of Hope, Healing & Joy"**. The ministry is currently reaching people across the nation each week. She is also the founder of Daughters of Zion Ministries, dedicated to serving women as they reach their true potential in God. She is a Prophet and an Anointed Dancer for the Lord.

She is a national financial education trainer and Financial Coach. She provides support to organizations and programs that empower families to build financial literacy skills, improve credit scores, access safe financial products, attain assets that create economic mobility and build generational wealth. During her career, she has trained over 2000 people across the nation and over 300 Financial Coaches. She has managed over $25 Million supporting over 20,000 families in homeownership, higher education, quality childcare, microenterprise business development, creating emergency savings accounts, and assisting low to moderate income to get their tax prepared for free. She is also the Founder of God's Economy, which is focused on financial empowerment in the faith community. Ms. Jackson has a BS from the New York Institute of Technology and resides in Atlanta GA.

She is most honored that God blessed her to be the mother of the late Edward J. Jackson III. Her only child that went to be with the Lord at age 20 in 2012.

My personal mission in life:
To live a life that exhibits the power of God working through me as I experience the learning moments, the trials, and the celebrations of my journey that will have a positive impact on the lives of others.

I Am God's Economy - Step Into Your Joy

Economy as a child

High School graduation 1982
Dwight Morrow High School

College graduation 1987
New York Institute of Technology

Jay Forever my Prince

Edward Jay Jackson, III – JJ The Prodigy

Rev. Economy (Connie McGee) F. Jackson
Minister, Motivational Speaker, Wedding Officiant, Retreat Facilitator, Anointed Dancer, Financial Education Instructor and Financial Coach

Bible Study: Every Tuesday at 8:00 PM Eastern Time. Just call 404.458.1835. 1 hour over the phone.

Morning Prayer: Every Wednesday at 6:30 AM. Just call 404.458.1835

Worship Service: Every Sunday at 9:00 AM on Facebook
www.facebook.com/TheRefreshingCenter

For more information or to share comments:
Email: TheRefreshingCenter@Gmail.com

Made in the USA
Columbia, SC
08 August 2023